400 YEARS
of WITNESSING

Dr. Molefi Kete Asante's *400 Years of Witnessing* will touch the core. These soul-stirring artistries of words such as *Ancestral Gathering, Oyo Reborn,* and *I Call for Oduduwa in the Belly of Odin* are POWERFUL! They illicit prayers, and manifest goosebumps of spiritual awakening. This book is a brilliant continuation of Dr. Molefi Kete. Asante's valued contributions to the Afrocentric paradigm and creates another avenue to grow through Afrocentricity.

—KENZOE BRIAN (OYAME) SELASSIE-OKPE, PHD

400 YEARS *of* WITNESSING

A Memoir of a People
1619-2019

Molefi Kete Asante

Universal Write Publications LLC

No part of this publication may be reproduced in whole or in part, or stored in a retrieval system, or transmitted in any form or by any means, electronic, mechanical, photocopying, recording or otherwise, without written permission from the publisher, except in the case of newspapers, magazines and websites using quotations embodied in critical essays and reviews.

400 YEARS OF WITNESSING, A Memoir of a People—1619-2019

Copyright © 2019 Molefi Kete Asante

All rights reserved.

Molefi Kete Asante
'The right of Molefi Kete Asante to be identified as the author of this Work has been asserted by him/her in accordance with sections 77 and 78 of the Copyright, Designs and Patents Act 1988.'

Book Designer: AuthorSupport.com
Editor: KenZoe Brian (Oyame) Selassie-Okpe, PhD

For information: Website at www.UWPBooks.com

Publisher:

Universal Write Publications LLC
Mailing/Submissions Universal Write Publications LLC
421 8th Avenue, Suite 86 New York, NY 10116

ISBN-13: 978-0-9825327-8-2
ISBN-10: 0-9825327-8-4

*Humbly dedicated to the lonesome twenty
who came ashore at Point Comfort, Virginia, in 1619*

Contents

Preface   *xiii*

How it All Began   1

I Heard My Sister Say   3

Music Vanishes as Memory Diminishes   4

Echoes We Drown Out   5

Each One is Stronger than the Chains   6

March Down the River Side   7

The Master Songs   8

We Journeyed on Through Time   9

Winning   10

Running Fast   11

New Memory   12

Charlie Parker   13

Ancestral Gathering   14

Hang   16

African Wishes   17

Profile   18

The Mask People   19

Nat Turner and Bantu Steve Biko   20

So   22

Soon   23

Named and Not Named   24

They Soon Come   25

Oyo Reborn   26

Who Can See?   28

Scene in the South   29

When We Changed the Languages   30

We are One   31

We Wrestled in Water and Dust   32

Liberia came on our Minds   33

The Four Moments of the Sun   34

I Declared Deep in the Cotton Fields of Georgia   35

Josiah Henson   36

Sojourner Truth   37

What is Ogun to do?   38

Harriet Tubman   40

High John the Conqueror Meets Ephraim M'ikiara   41

Deceit   43

We Keep Going North   44

The People of Jazz   45

Urban People   46

Advice   47

Forest Voice   48

Harlem Renaissance   49

Craving Freedom   50

Our House   51

As I See It   52

Manhood Stance   53

Who is Prepared to Tell the African Anything?   54

Plenty Smith Talking Knowledge   55

The Hound Dog   56

Freedom on the Other Side of the Line   57

Run, Run, Run for Your Life   58

Marcus Garvey   59

We Breathe a New Air   60

Soul   61

Lynching   63

A Thousand Nadirs   64

Poets Above the Fray   65

My Mind Goes Guinea Drunk   66

Running Away   67

Veterans   68

I Remember the Fields   69

Grief Came with Its Own Umbrella   70

Harriet Tubman Revisited   71

Emmett Till   72

Iba to the Revolutionaries   73

Casualties of American Wars   74

Tuskegee   75

Her Name was Mary McLeod Bethune   76

The Time Began   77

Great are the Gods   78

Clever   79

Heroic Mother Escaping   80

Scene and Not Seen   81

What We Shall Do?   82

The People are Gods   83

Veil   84

Courage Talk   85

Martin Luther King   86

If I Speak   87

Meeting My Lover across the Ohio River   88

Can You See?   89

Child Labor   91

Of People and Animals   92

Beauty as Beauty Does   93

Keeping me from Knowledge?   94

I Don't Feel Weary   95

Depression Years   96

On Reading   97

My Running   98

Brutishness   99

Pivoting in the Fields of a Thousand Obstacles   100

Entry   102

Captured and Held   103

Dungeons Memory   104

Ship   105

Crossing   106

Strength   107

A Moment   108

Landed   109

Thinking   110

Beginning   111

Walking in Shackles   112

On the Auction Block   113

And Now We Must Go On   114

The Brave Never Left Us   115

Egun Memories   116

Night Escape   117

Elevation   118

Sold Down the River   119

Forty Acres and a Mule   120

Initiated in the Sea   121

Should I Forget?   123

What Greed?   124

I Remember the Path   125

Epic Dance   127

Rhythms of Africa   128

Detached   129

Knowing Reincarnation   130

I Call for Oduduwa in the Belly of Odin   132

On Arrival in Pennsylvania   134

Fannie Lou Hamer   135

Poets   136

Resistance then   137

In the Cities   138

Victory over Insanity   139

Strangers Still   140

Homage to Musical Genius   141

The Church of St. John the Coltrane   142

Rosewood   143

When Freedom Came   144

Malcolm X   145

Young Bucks' Mysteries   146

Frederick Douglass   147

Mother of the Universe   148

Liberty and Freedom   149

54th Massachusetts Glorified   150

Martin Delany   151

Frame of Reference   152

A Thousand Miles with Chains   153

Abandoned?   154

Home Always on My Mind   155

Prediction   156

Preface

These poems are my memoir of a people. I have not lived a quarter of our sojourn in this country, but I have observed enough, read enough, talked enough, and experienced enough to know something of our witness as we have engaged the remnants of the English colony known as the United States of America.

This book is about racism and our antagonism toward it as we have tried to make this country a better place for all people. Our frame of mind from the beginning was resistance to racial domination and we tried every way that we could, to insure the strong children would soon come and stop the business of racial brutality. Some claim that we are resilient and there is truth to that acknowledgment, but we are also resisters and that is the story that is told in this poetic memoir.

I have to count myself fortunate to have the words and thoughts of our illustrious ancestors come through me to commemorate four hundred years of sterling battles against the most cruel, barbarous, and pathetic people Africans have ever encountered. Of course, there may be others viler, and more obscene, but we only know the ones who stole us from Africa and worked us nearly to death. Yet in our mind and body were written the DNA of survival and victory and few people in adversity have found as many brave and courageous women and men as have Africans in America.

I have written like our history, free, episodic, diachronic, passionate, and genuine with no sense of chronology to give the reader the true situation with our battles everywhere. We are not isolated on islands, but our struggle has been against all institutions, every organization, and many groups and individuals who have shown the most heinous side of humanity although we have done nothing, not a thing, to prompt the irrationality that we have seen.

One could think of many avenues for commemoration of the 400 Years of Witnessing, but for me, this quadricentennial called up the poetic voices deep in my soul. I have often written poetry, hundreds of poems, although I have only published two books of poetry in my career. It is a severe discipline, and I have always found myself wrestling with the meaning of poetic art. Thus, three years ago I started the journey of writing a book of poems to ritualize the commemoration.

Poetry, for me, is informed art. It is clear that poetry that uninformed is shapeless, that is, without form. I wanted to write art and I knew that it could not be art without being formed, created to reflect the depth of the African's journey in America. Knowing and experiencing as well as reflecting and meditating on the history, literature, and music of the people would give me form and information. I have studied and written history for many years and I have found my artistic references past and present with a projection to the future to be shaped by the classic examples in our history. In one sense I am an artist and even in my writing of these poems the art remains inside me. The production of these poems are creations of form grounded in every type of knowledge. One cannot be a poet or any kind of writer of art without knowledge; otherwise there is no discipline. For example, versification without knowledge is not necessarily poetry. Indeed, things lovely may not be poetic. We live among people who are pleased by cruelties and deformities but this cannot be confused with either art or poetic art.

What I have done is to ornament these creations with language that emblemizes our 400 years of resistance and resilience. I have worked to make these poems, a memoir of a people, function for us in a metaphysical-magical manner to ritually activate transformation in a spiritual sense. I use the myths, the universe, the narratives of courage, the proverbs, the ancient wisdom of sage women and men, to attach the brilliance of these acts of creation to our yearnings for authenticity and victories over insanity. In some cases you will see that I have tried to reinvent or resurrect icons that have been forgotten or lost in generational shifts. Let it be understood, however, that it can never be ornament for the sake of ornament. When ornament, whether figures, metaphors, or similes, are no longer understood writing becomes sophistry. I present these poems as an effort to keep alive forever the memories of the indomitable ones.

These poems, filled with iconic signs and deep passionate words, are therefore not angry poems but they are confident as the people are confident, and resilient as the people are resilient, and victors as we are and will ever be with the assistance of the ancestors whose names we call in this book.

How it All Began

Shalafia!
Nagadef?
Jambo!
Wo ho te sen?

Languages I did not know,
song in rhythmic voices
Tones unknown to me
in words distant from my ears.

Nothing like my Bamileke, Baluba, Ijaw, or Ibibio
Danced in conversations that must have been like mine

What is the meaning of this?
Who are these bizarre creatures
who stare when they see me?

Where does this pinkness
belong in our great universe?

Why would strangers not greet
the ancestors as they enter?

What are the invisible spears
they use to kill our royal leaders?

Where are they taking us,
Without asking us if we want to go?

This is the way it began, this long journey,
With no certain destination but confusion.

I wired my body and mind with ancestors' strength
Counting the names of generations gone,
I prepared my soul to ride the wind without fear.
I bring you now the results of four hundred years
Of fearlessness, of *kujichagulia, imani,* and purpose.
Go nowhere, move to no other space, be here and hear
   the voices of four hundred years gathered in one place.

I Heard My Sister Say

Of course, I know that their intent is cruelty
But I will not be a penned lamb in their slaughter
I shall resist forever the naked brutality
Like a finely dressed and present daughter.
They will never know my honored name
Because it is concealed in ancestral history
Far away from these shores to which we came
Keeping for me a form of ancestral mystery.

Music Vanishes as Memory Diminishes

We grew up on dancers and drummers
Playing the sounds of our ancestors
And even moved to the *kete* and *fontom from*,
Our feet flying lightly on the sacred sand
Running to our own distant land
Like High John de Conqueror.
Yes, we grew up on drummers and dancers
Only to bury their sounds and rhythms
In the cadences of the cane and cotton
Standing in the thousands of lonesome fields.
Of course, we were not made for strange deeds.
We were not born to wear the chain of the enslaved
And so we have spent our four centuries righting,
Fighting the senseless stupidity of race terror.

Echoes We Drown Out

In the faces of the masses,
Children of David Walker,
Who walk by day,
 shadowed by night
passing the witch's broom,
We sing Arawak and Taino praises
And plant starred *veves*
on the ground,
in the crevices of our brains
Crowding out reason, some say,
leaving space for laced emotions,
Threaded from memories of many gone.
Just hear the voices cry out,
Just move to Ogun's drums becoming
Exhausted, limp like a lifeless fish,
We are unable to speak or to explain.
Yet like the violent crack of whips
The thunder and lightning move
In passionate tunes
To the rhythms of life
And we sing for heaven's mercy-
Only to wake up in hell's despair.

Each One is Stronger than the Chains

Circling colors of rainbows
With small and large centers
Merge into the blueness of my head
Sadness so deep one could drown
Pours from within my soul
And I grow morose
Devoid of place and time
Like a whiff of an artist's brush
Off on the horizon, but
I will not be an afterthought!

March Down the River Side

We walked for four days through shards
of broken promises
Minds racing faster than the crows could fly
As our feet fell in unison to the beat of dust
And we vowed like the people we are
That we would never cut our flesh on the shards
Crushed and splayed before us like piercing knives.
Hundreds made the walk with us,
Then thousands came
And in the end millions who followed
Dodged and leaped the pieces of broken dreams
And we found hope in resilient deftness.
Reaching New Orleans after four days of woe,
we sang and danced in the Mississippi River
Where I heard the majestic sacred songs
Ringing from the chambers of Marie Laveau.

The Master Songs

I heard them first at my mother's knee,
Purer sound than any angel could make.
Majesty bolder than any sonnet or song
The human ear had ever entertained,
These master songs draped the human voice
With a grandeur of the most elaborate passion
Of the unquenchable longing for our home.

We Journeyed on Through Time

Maligned by time and shortchanged by space
We contested both space and time.
Triumphant ambers of dying courage
Reawaken with each generation
Willing to light the fires of ancestral wood
Sparked science, and art, and dance, and philosophy

And Langston appeared next to Ellison and Wright,
Up popped Toni Morrison and James Baldwin and Rita Dove
Joining Madhubuti, Sanchez, Baraka, and Mari Evans,
And the ambient compromises disappeared in art.

Winning

I chant the forty-two confessions
I chant the Shabaka legend
I chant the Kebra Negast
I chant the ode to Ogun
I chant the Zulu Declaration
I take up the machete of Carlota
I take up the spear of Kenyatta
I take up the sword of Dessalines
I take the baton of the queen of Leogane
I take up the knife of Nat Turner
I take up the shotgun of Harriet Tubman
I disdain arrogance
I disdain pride
I disdain dishonesty
I disdain greed
I disdain narcissism
I disdain discrimination
I use the gift of oratory to denounce evil
I use the gift of poetry to announce beauty
I use the gift of speech to lash the unethical
I am the glue that holds the concrete together
I am the glue that pretzeled the nation into truth
I am the one who frustrates the liars
I seek nothing more than freedom.
I refuse to be nothing but free!

Running Fast

We run on the brownest leaves
Strewn about in autumn's light
On the path through glazed fear
As the hounds barked
Our feet took us to the air
With tropic's thoughts
As we escaped once more the lair.

New Memory

Oshun and Yemanja sing,
We listen to the resounding
Music like gurgling rivers,
Turbulent oceans, splendid chords,
Of memories corporeal.

We people the Americas
Plant our seeds in the Caribbean
And vow to remember ancestors
Whose surreal presence we need
And whose constant spirits ring!

Charlie Parker

Bop bop be bop be bop
De de de de de de
Saybo say bo saybo saybo
Hey hey hey hey hey
Bom um bom um bom
Bom um bom um bom
La la la la la la la
Ah la ah la ah la ah la
La la la bog la la bog
Uh la uh la uh la uh la
Oooe oooe oooe oooe
Trying to get to
Ara-niyi or ara owo
O woe!
Seeking the rhythms of bop
In the realm of Hip Hop
I linger in the background
Long enough to catch my breath
Like a log coming to life
I snatch freedom in my
Moments of reflection
Like a crocodile eager to eat
Muddy words that ring with truth
And darkened words that cater
To the innermost thoughts
Of a people going from sad to mad,
Only to rise in joy later!

Ancestral Gathering

(intoned to kongas)

David Walker
Come on down
Nat Turner
Come on down
Patrice Lumumba
Come on down
Denmark Vesey
Come on down
Edward Mondlane
Come on down
Malcolm X
Come on down
Martin Luther King
Come on down
Harriet Tubman
Come on down
Medgar Evers
Come on down
Elijah Muhammad
Come on down
Sojourner Truth
Come on down
Kwame Ture
Come on down
John Henrik Clarke
Come on down
Queen Mother Moore

Come on down!
Twenty Africans at Point Comfort in 1619 on my mind
Richard Allen in 1793 is on my mind
Sojourner Truth in 1827 running away is on my mind
Mary Turner 1917 brutalized is on my mind
Tulsa 1921 is on my mind
Birmingham 1963 is on my mind
Medgar Ever l963 is on my mind
Thousands hung on trees, and
Murdered youth before their prime
Come on down!

Hang

Hang
It was not necessary
For us to hang
Without dropping
Without crying
Without dying
It was not necessary

Pens point to lies
Beneath the surfaces
Of executioner's skins
And we hang tough
Because
It was not necessary
It was not enough
To drop
To cry
To die
We must chew up ropes
We must burn nooses
We are not fetishes
In white America.
We are sacred ebony
Rich with melanin
Magic wands that can turn out lights
And make festival time anytime.
We are separate and apart,
One all the same,
 At the same time.

African Wishes

Thiatou is far away
I passed it along the way
With shadows following
My presence rolling along the line
Chains clinking
Children clinging
Lingering bleakness dimmed the day
And Tamaschek camps appear
Longest in my memory
As my mother's journey, so long,
Torches my torched spirit
And muffled voices of ancestors
Whistle with the wind
Near the barren rock crater caves
As I become the lion of the lines.

Profile

I am tall, black and male
I walk the streets refusing to fear
That I could end up in jail
Just because I am tall, black, and male.

I am young and active in sports
Making my debut as a referee
But I could be whipped and killed
Simply because I am feel free.

Remember me when you hear
The name of the young black man
Caught on tape arrested for singing
On the streets while being black.

The Mask People

We are the mask people of Carolina
We wear our hearts
On rattan
Our faces are dark red black
Like the cosmos
And we wear masks
That tell everything
That we need to know about love and life
Because we are mask people
Making unreality real
And making real what is and has been
Lowland Negroes they call us
And we smile beneath our masks.

Nat Turner and Bantu Steve Biko

In the hidden lands of sick minds
White madness
Spreading its deathly fear
From petal to petal
Hoping to crush
Our blossoming flower
Killed Steve Biko.

Diamonds and gold
With veins of history
Witnessed the cry
And saw the insanity
Sailing from Europe
With cannibal hearts
That attacked Steve Biko

Talking trees,
Walking mountains
Cursed the nocturnal stealth
That beat, stomped and abused
The frightening manhood of Steve Biko
 with grimy bloody white hands.
Vile with bluish pinkness
their tongues spit out Viking venom
and shot Dutch's daggers at Biko.

Our wonder child
Like his Pan African siblings
Conscious, black, and all powerful

Would reap the revenge
That would be freedom from fear of death.
A delicate intellectual in jail,
A scientific mind
Sense talking brother
Activist in life for peace and justice
Now dead, assassinated in a police van,
After abuse
In a South African cell.

Like Nat Turner, who went before him,
He made suns shine
And lit full black moons
When he thundered in political whispers
What had to be done
He made us think right
And made us think, right,
And made us think and do, right?
Right!

So

Where questions arise
Questions are answered
In the universe of time

When girls with yellow shoes
Stroll behind mothers
Who wear no shoes,
And fathers
Who sing the blues,
While scouring for food
In the meadows of Georgia,
Questions arise,
So?

Soon

We were eager to learn
Roaring into centuries ahead of time
Willing to understand radical lines
From Keynes and even Marx
Drunk with the drug of knowing
We elevated our intellect

But no deeds we have done
Have ever yet begun
To redress our mental occupation
And calmed our revolutionary situation

What good for half of us
To break through to the sun
And the rest of us
 remain tragically undone?

Named and Not Named

Like a cotton silk memory
Tall and straight as a Wolof
I stood in bas relief
On the side of a slick mountain
Leaning barefoot against rock
Deep in reason
Drowning in clamoring thoughts
About
Benin, Samory Ture, Cayor,
Amadu Bamba, Yenenga, Nzingha,
Sundiata, Sumanguru, and my Amiru

Gone are the voices of yesterday
And now labor without reward
And now abhorrent and crass people
Waited for me below in Tennessee's valley.

I regained my footing
Brushed off my coarse sack shirt
headed down the valley
where kings would rise
With diadems of bullets.
I knew kings would come
And break the discord
And peace would be still, stiller
Than the rock I borrowed.

They Soon Come

When will the kings and queens,
Do their thing?

Fly from Juba land
And bring *lucumi*

Fling their Guinea fists
And battle the devils

On the land and in my mind,
When will they come?

Oyo Reborn

I would see a tall lanky man
With curly hair
And skin yellow like white
Vow to rebuild Oyo

I listen but I keep moving

My thoughts are eagles
They ride quickly to Africa
Where Oyo rose from the forest

I am tired of fighting
But I will not give up
Until I see Oyo reborn
In the forests of South Carolina

When I see Oyo reborn
With lines of descent etched on my face
Like the scarifications of Ife,
Long, long, long ago
I will shout Obatala and Ogun
I will shout Oshun and Yemaja

Like the revolution of bodies
In motion I move in the dust
Of the streets with rhythmic feet
Joined with others who dance
In the grand union of *orishas*

Yes, I have seen Oyo reborn
In sculpted black memories
leaning against old wooden fences
encapsulated by knowing nothing
But now know Eshu and Shango
Singing Olorun's anthem;' at Oyo Tunji.

Who Can See?

Through the world of Benin bronzes
Ivory men heads and Dogon *nommos*
Duke Ellington can see
Miles Davis can see
John Coltrane can see
Nina Simone can see

Eyes open wide
With no glare casting gloom
Over the stories of victories
Gained day by day by millions
Who could not see!

Yet they wandered
Covered in their blackness
Toward the light
Where jazzmen could see

They see notes in the black
They see rhythms in the dust
They metronome in their souls
I can hear the notes they see
And my ears become eyes.

Scene in the South

Royal entourages in rags
Drag queens across the land
And send kings to tobacco fields
Singing and dancing in reds and greens
Their black bodies swaying,
Occasionally saying proverbs.

When We Changed the Languages

Aime Cesaire changed the French language
Alexander Pushkin blackened Russian
Langston Hughes made English sing
Nicolas Guillen captured Spanish,
Their poetry added soul to prose,
To languages languishing in narration,
Dunbar announced a new translucent lyric
Sung by Tupac and J-Z through the prism
Of Baraka, Mari Evans, and Sonia Sanchez.

We are One

The Baluba are a nation of poets
The Kongo are their sisters and brothers
The Ndebele dance all night to poetry
The Zulu are they relatives
The Yoruba speak ancient proverbs
The Benis and Igbo sing alongside them
They are from the same source!

We Wrestled in Water and Dust

There was a silence in the tone
A moving image of clocks marking time
Through the years like the sound of corn
Grinding slowly in water
Like an old man snoring away the years.
Yet we children of the midnight stars
Splashed in water and rustled banana leaves
Wrestling like Nubians in the dust,
With the sound of rushing feet
Trampling on all verbal negations
Until the young children awake and smile.

Liberia came on our minds

Liberia ushered forth like a gush of fresh air in a stale coach
Intent on bringing freedom everywhere for us
Who were slammed into a backseat bondage,
Whipped and abused by dog-eared overseers
Doing the bidding of lucifers in white pants.

We bumped fists and slapped backs and raised hands
High above our heads while singing hallelujahs
Just like freedom had returned to Africa's land.
Like a tornado of putrid air in an open room full of play
Hate and bitterness erupted in strong ethnic tones
And we fought in the street like mad dogs
Like we had not been born by the same mother.

The Four Moments of the Sun

A twist of light laced by the moon
Like sunrays across our countenance
We glitter in our velvet dusk

Children of the Middle Passage,
We, the harvest of remnant rays
Join a beam of history
And like the four moments of the sun

Converge to dance to the rhythms
Of light bursting through the night.

I Declared Deep in the Cotton Fields of Georgia

I declare allegiance to Maat
I delve into its most magical secrets
I discover myself raising my own djed
   Like the ancients who told truth.

My declarations are like those of David Walker
Bent by the experiences of neglect
Shaped in the crucibles of sacrifice,
Yet I cannot forget my responsibility to Maat
It has twisted my attitude into its tight knot
Made me invulnerable to the arrows of hell.

I salute Maat, the beautiful golden woman of Africa,
And rise to greet children who praise her noble head.

Josiah Henson

I spent forty years
Shuffling for the white man on a Maryland plantation
While lodging in a damp, cold, smoky log hut.
In this one room with barren sod floor
I sat to eat food with ten others,
Mothers, fathers, and siblings
Huddled like frozen wet cattle in a corner for heat,
Laying on straw, under a single holy blanket,
Stretched over several frigid bodies,
I vowed to escape, killing the enslaver, if I had to.

Sojourner Truth

Am I not a woman?
Am I not a human?
The white man threw me into a buck
Tied my hands together
Forced me to squat down
Ran a stick behind my knees
And in front of my elbows
With my knees up against my breasts.
My hands were tied together
Just in front of my shins
Holding me in what they called a buck.
I was whipped on one side till it bled
Turned over on the other, and whipped to a pulp.
Torn up and crippled, bruised and debased
I promised my ancestors slavery would end.

What is Ogun to Do?

When the sun shards turn blue
And the earth is green-gone
Will you see what I told you?
Will you hear better
Or does it matter to you
That sun-roses blossom
That moon-lanterns glow
That star-seeds mature
Right before your pallid eyes?

A notion occurred unnoticed
And the forest crept away
Silently it stole into a hidden lay.
Can you smell its tree-scent?
Glass grew where grass spent
Sand drank milk water
And you say you missed it
Saw it not,
Heard it not,
Smelled it not,
Felt it not?

Sure, you see the unnatural signs
Dropping in and out of sight
Like, hey, KKK, and
OK ephemeral you may say
But what is Ogun to do
When the sun shards turn blue
And the earth is green-gone

And the Blue Jay is songless
And the child freezes in adults
And the heat burns nothing?

Harriet Tubman

I had reasoned dis in my mind
Dat I had a right to two things:
I had a right to liberty
I had a right to death
If I could not have one
I would have the other.

High John the Conqueror Meets Ephraim M'ikiara

Who can fly like High John de Conqueror?
Tell me why
Ephraim M'ikiara cannot fly.

Fly Ephraim fly
Fly in the night
Fly with all might

High John de Conqueror can ride the wind
Ephraim can count the steps
Up the steep glacier,
They both can fly at will

Warrior boulders could not stop Ephraim
Bloodhounds could not stop High John

We say fly Ephraim fly
Fly to the top
Fly and fly

Find High John the Conqueror
At Africa's crown
covered with tie-dyed fabrics
made from cotton we picked in Georgia
Fly Ephraim fly to the sky!
Like a firefly fly
Lighting the grey-gloom

Prophesies of doom
You reach the earth-moon
Greet your god in peace
Autograph the lease,
Activate blessings for another year

High John can fly
Fly on high
Far to the sky
Like Ephraim can fly
Beyond Kenya's top.

Deceit

Shango danced in my head
And memories slashed by
When night stumbled on white lies
Cold like eyeless terror
Ignominiously celebrated
I bit the iron
Ogun took my oath
And orishas saddled me with
All the protection I needed
Rainbows appeared bold
Undeceived and Undeceivable!

We Keep Going North

Running and walking
Scared of the silence heard inside our hearts
We burst forth
Like blazing jacarandas
Spread out across the forest

We are men and women
Loops and staffs
We are pure indigo
Changed into bright reds and oranges
Spilling into freedom

The People of Jazz

Spirits soaring northward
To the indomitable rhythms
Of a *Fontonfrom* and *Kete*
Talking to fleeting ancestors
Nearer and farther away
Where deep strong basses and baritones and tenors
Name a rhythmic gluon
Of signals for ebony souls
Straight into a heaven meant for deep emotions
To question our own spirits.

They honor unnamed princes
In Viking lands
Where the people never understood or really heard
A Coltrane or a Milesian warrior mad with genius
Or ever saw a Bird gliding or a Duke reigning jazz.

Our gift from our god
Our star-flowers budding open
Our treasure-hearts bounding with percussive energy
Our honey-genius playing the cool Celestial music.

Urban People

I surveyed the stone and steel
The brick and iron
The wood and clay
The aluminum and glass
And felt good
Knowing like Pac and JZ
That my genius
And my toil
Were responsible for everything I saw.

Advice

Put steel in your tongue
You'll need it

Chew brass kola nuts
You'll need them, too.

The *Congressional Quarterly*
Is a windy mausoleum

Put African uranium
In your American briefcases

Make a pact with Chaka
And cancel the Quarterly today.

Forest Voice

Palm groves grow
In the thickets of my confused brain
I hang a Baule mask
From the giant among them
And weaverbirds
Uncharacteristically
Fly from limb to limb
Weaving a Sankofa
Summoning
Me to listen to my own ancestors
On a moon painted night
Sparkling with blackness
I wandered down a Lenox Avenue
And found Malcolm X talking
To Asa Hilliard
In the divine language of Kemet
Resurrected and generative
With a thousand stretched *Nommo* hands
High in the sky
Marking the resetting of the clock
Of our ancestry.
Do you know what time it is?

Harlem Renaissance

On a damp red moonlit evening
Gray with suspicion
I strolled along Seventh Avenue
Somewhere in America.

A flame, ambient in color,
Burns yellow now
Smoke rises over houses
Constructed with blood

Radiance distills
I see a child
Slip on a banana peel

Running

On a moon painted night'
Sparkling with blackness
As I strolled the Avenue
I found Claude McKay, Countee Cullen,
Zora Neale Hurston, Langston Hughes
And W. E. B. eating grits, reading, and drinking coffee
At Arturo Schomburg's corner store.

Up walked little Richard Wright with littler James Baldwin
Singing verses written by Margaret Walker for my people.
I stopped, checked the date and time, and went further uptown
To ask Alain Locke to reset the clock for the New Negro.

Craving Freedom

Eating clay and spitting juices
She sang of prophets
She honored the god of reproduction
She climbed the ladder of wisdom

Chewing pine needles
Her thoughts turned to children
Her meditations on loss
Her eyes draped with sadness
Spoke Ogun's resilience

Traveling by foot
The days were longer than usual
Too many stories told
Too many jokes made
Yet she persisted as we persist.

We have craved as she had craved
For freedom and our eyes saw in a twinkle
Something that we could never forget
Traveling by decades in lightning speed
We captured what we know she wanted.

Our House

Valleys and ridges in the raw earth
Brushed to perfection
Like in Haiti
Like in Jamaica
Like in Congo
Like in Angola
Like in Bwasola
Like in Benin
Like in Guadeloupe
Like in Ghana
That was our front yard
Twirling platforms,
Stages for dancing and prancing
deep into the bristling night.

As I See It

Swords and guns
Churches and ammo shops
Overlooking Black Bottom

Eagles perched on pillars
Of red, white and blue
Stones faced brownness boiling
With ropes hanging in waiting
While we escape again and again.

Manhood Stance

Tears danced down his cheek
A man he was at fourteen
Heat went to sleep at noon
And he was cold, so cold
In the 'terrogation' room

What had he done,
Except speak up when asked
What he thought about the killing?

Only frost occupied his space
And the coldness, palpable
Beyond his young Georgia days
Struck emotionless
Like carbon monoxide
To snuff the warmth out of him.

Who is Prepared to Tell the African Anything?

Rachet up the snow flowers
Shut down the red chimneys
Of Saint Nicholas,
Substitute green for purple
Let the slow narratives begin
Capturing gross tonnage of filth
From the rhetoric of politicians

We are not cowered by tongues
Slagging slut and moving moisture
From cotton to tobacco
Or masquerading with fronds
As maggot frowns sleazy with death

When what we have seen in this land
Is blood from the nose of Liberty's Statue,
Who is prepared to tell us any *thing*
Or to remind us of humanity?

Plenty Smith Talking Knowledge

I knew symbols but could not read
I felt the squares and circles by nature,
I could discern the evil or the good in others,
But Nat Turner had opened my eyes wide
I was woke when he explained the mysteries
That whites could also bleed and die.

The Hound Dog

And there it is once more
The old hound dog that wanders our street
Painted in the setting light of the sun
A cruel unremembered gray
Unlike the time when whites rode alongside him
In search of black flesh hot on the trail

Now there are no adages awaiting
No rewarding fixes of duck meat
No celebratory shouting and laughing
No naked or near naked black women bodies
No naked or near naked black male asses
Groveling in the sand at the feet of slave catchers

Like something out of the distant past
Long ago in the ignorant ages of yesteryear
When catching black bodies was not football
The hound dog, with a brushed auburn look,
Shared the ignominious stage with murderers
And now wanders our streets long forgotten.

Freedom on the Other Side of the Line

I stumble
Shuffle footed across the horizon line
With boldness like a Shakan soldier
Upright like an Iroko tree
Standing
But aware of the fading sun
Falling quickly toward the way crossed
On the last day of bondage.
Free at last!

Run, Run, Run for your Life

Frames with oily essence terrorize
Scents hounded by lay gunmen hunting
Bodies black by the day's light
Moving with the speed of fright

Gifted with sheets of courage living
On edges of madness with hisses of fear
Strained vocal chords tear at the source
To give voice to the patient voiceless

I am John Henry driving steel through hell
Shine spitting throaty saliva at murderers,
Simple simply reciting forgotten verses
Slipping the hang person's ropes again.

Marcus Garvey

If in life you find me bitter,
In death I shall be a greater terror
Cause I shall inspire generations of fighters
Whose aim shall be nothing but victory,
This I give to you as a predictory!

We Breathe a New Air

Auxiliaries of agitation grope for air
Unbreathable because of history's pain
Yet muddled in the fire brands of hatred

Climbing sewages of wasted flesh
Spilling over into insanity
Hurting and not relenting in freedom

We are the ones who speak for peace
Crippled it might be
Chokeholded to death on an island

Always we, pure as coal, claim
The air like everyone
And rise up to breathe a new breath.

Soul

Radical child bent harmony out of the ethereal space made pure
Trudging onward with caned blossoms of strawed toughness,
Sifting the innermost and truculent wills like pressed blackberries,
Whose juices are as sweet as a mother's eye on a wayward offspring.

The blood of a thousand earths caked up in the testes of hell
Unfrozen in us and we danced across four hundred years of madness
Stoned with grace willed to us in volcanic thrusts by gods of destiny
Fraught with faint licenses yielding pathos deep throated and real

Bunches of lean trunks bending at the elbows near where the
    leaves are,
Sway like home's palms waving incessantly to the next generation
We are the inevitable ones, stalked by the damned roving trouble,
    yet free
With stains of blood leached into our consciousness like Ethiopia's caffeine.

Sacred flues extract poisons from our souls and ushers in fresh styles
Colored with textures of rainbows and shaped like ripples in water,
We who have removed shit from our rhythmic feet for four
    hundred years
Need no petty instructions from unseen gods about keeping our shoes
    clean.

Caught between the edges of deceit and greed the sharpness quicks
Like petrol burning in the Nigerian delta and I run shaking like a tree
Unable to coil like a cocoon and roll in the sand of southern plains
I stand impregnable, a baobab with arms held open ready to fly

It is not imaginary, something ethereal, unreal, and barely faint
Darkness comes in cycles like the seasons in the temperate zones
Deeper than Eredo's trench, thicker than Bwasola's rainforest
Painted on my skin, smoother than the juice of ripe mangoes

I leap a lion jump clawed onto history and soaked in music
Stuck clearly in the memory of ancestors casting about on ships
Bound for the ignominy led by the gutted hollows of men
Too afraid to dance and be recognized as decent in Shango's company

Yet I escaped, and harnessed history with the reins of my will
Cracked the robotic code of time and introduced the pathos of soul.
I had walked upright longer, taught pride earlier, and lifted the
    pyramids
To the blue umbrella while filling the universe with baskets of axes

Distributed from generation to generation like flowers to victors,
Petals of memory and power strengthen the weary feet of people so
    bold
To stare down fear and resurrect anger dead in centuries of shame,
Ogun marches with Itapua's Yemanja from palmed land to
    Afric's shore.

Exhausted from anticipation I pivot from weakness to strength,
I clasp alabaster vases of power gathered from generations in
    both hands,
I hasten to sing Eshu's music before the evening's shadows cast
    their spells;
I stamp the quadricentennial complete and raise a *tekken* to
    begin anew.

Lynching

I bring to the gallows only myself
Innocent and unafraid of death,
But frightened for the life of my children
And their mothers, whom I love.
A thousand scenes drum their way into my brain
With images of red, white, and blue signs of murder.
As I stand, solitary, waiting, on the scaffolds
With truth besides me, with justice on my side
I could have pleaded, begged, and cried,
But I wait for the brusque hangman's noose
Around my strong black neck,
Confidently knowing that in death
I shall conquer my enemies with my children.

A Thousand Nadirs

Self-resurrection from a thousand nadirs.
Bowed often, beaten without reason,
Pummeled as if nothing in the world cared,
Yet I collected my strength like little seeds of gold
To be shared with others out of luck and in the cold

Poets Above the Fray

Whose star rose when poets were born?
Are we poets rich or poor by the stars?
Or do we ride in chariots near the dusk
Of anonymous horizons
Like Melvin B. Tolson's
Libretto for the Republic of Liberia?

My Mind Goes Guinea Drunk

No darkness exceeds that of Guinea
It is neither purple nor blue,
Neither red nor yellow
But a splendorous keeper of history.
And when I think deeply
I can see Guinea in my imagination
Comforting, convenient, consuming;
And I fall down, prostrate, in prayer
Drunk with Guinea thinking!

Running Away

I become invisible in the night
I run like the gazelle
I swim like the fish
I fly like the eagle
I become invisible in the night
But in the daylight,
I am eternally present.

Veterans

The men, unbounded birds without time or rule,
Sing on the cold streets of urban America
Their tired songs of disappointment and shame,
Voices angry, aggressive as flying ants,
Swarm indifference on the freezing streets,
And pedestrians walk fast, looking back.

Charles Fuller waves a flag to flag them down
So that they can hear a soldier's story!

They see Cathay Williams, serving as a man,
Her womanliness hidden under camouflage
At the battle of Pea Ridge in uncivil times.
They see brave William Harvey Carney
Saving the regimental colors at Fort Wagner
Where Yoruba, Igbo, Bamileke lost their lives
Sacrificing that me and you could walk free.
They see Henry O. Flipper graduating West Point
After running the bitter racial obstacle course,
They see Benjamin O. Davis Sr., Brigadier General,
And his son Benjamin O. Davis, Jr., Tuskegee's ace
Who commanded the never-losing pilots of destiny.
They see Dorie Miller, farm boy from Waco,
A messman third class, whose anti-aircraft wizardry
From the deck of the USS West Virginia
Inspired a people from New York to San Francisco.
Everywhere they look at long black veterans walking
They see bravery un-assaulted by fear and valor aglow.

I Remember the Fields

I remember the smell of cassava cooking
And the anticipation of spicy sauce
Like the breath of my mother,
Warm and caressing, moist with affection.
I remember that I am strong like the bamboo
Resilient and straight while facing the wind,
I share crop and drop in the sandy rows of cotton
But I remember, and I rise like the Bennu.

Grief Came with Its Own Umbrella

I sensed that evil had taken over
It gripped our shotgun house like a vise
Squeezed down upon our emotions
And we were sunk into the ocean of tears
When they said, "He'll never be the same."

My mother's life would continue
But her light would be dimmed by the news
That the white doctor in the segregated hospital
Had operated on the wrong spinal discs.

I choked, the oldest son, my siblings sighed
And cried, but nothing seemed to help
In the bitter moment when we saw him.
Our dad entered the two-bedroom house
Dragging one foot and then the other
Like a man handling inanimate sacks of coal,
then he smiled, broadly and said, "I'm back."

His smile was an umbrella for our grief.

Harriet Tubman Revisited

The lazy land of the Eastern Shore of Maryland conceals its horrors
Under the guise of "southern hospitality" toward white traders
And genteel brutalities like a thousand pins into our black flesh.

Her name was Harriet, so young, so brave, and daring
In her quest for freedom she climbed the ladder of courage
Found will, nobility, and leadership sitting on top,
Took them with grace and grit to lead us out of bondage.

Emmett Till

He threw no javelins, made no fist;
They entered his sleeping room
While he lay on his bed at rest,
Only a child of fourteen at most

Like wild bears of the steppes
They hit him, choked him, stomped him,
Tore at his flesh with claws of death
And when he was a mess of blood

They dumped his mangled body
In its disfigured, maimed state
Into the bronze Tallahatchie River;
But the watery grave gave up its dead.

He was martyred Emmett Till
Identified by his initialed ring;
His name still to us like a sacrificed ram
Shrieking in the dusk of many dawns.

Iba to the Revolutionaries

My eyes were lasers piercing every phenomenon,
Penetrating the slightest injustice,
Searing antagonisms and watching Time.
When I should have been the head of my clan
Satisfied with my wives and children
Wotan's son smashed my dignity under his feet,
Mashed it, ground it into the fabric of his society.
Raped my wife and daughters, sodomized my sons.
And then Time suddenly appeared bold and clear as day.
And there I stood between life and death
Choosing death over enslavement, I slit Wotan's throat.

Casualties of American Wars

Who threw away my brothers slipping and sliding down in the gutters
Of stone and steel monster cities who eat men and spit them
 in sewers?
How did the lizards of not knowing when or where, surround
 my brothers
Just done fighting in Germany, France, Italy, Guam, Korea, Vietnam
 and Afghanistan and Iraq?
Who stole their beautiful African souls full of peace diamonds,
And crippled their brains and left them decrepit beggars in alleyways?

How shall our families survive without the healthy wholeness we
 once knew?
As winter follows autumn and spring follows winter, surely
 summer comes
When we shall resurrect the dying from endless insomnias and
 amnesias
And return their diamonds with therapeutic shots of heady history
Long forgotten in the dens of wars and the pits of depraved racial
 trenches.

Tuskegee

I saw Booker T. take that axe and fell that tree,
Tuskegee was wilderness then and if campus it was to be
It would take scores of men and women free
To study, to cook, to read, to recite, and sail the sea.

Her Name was Mary McLeod Bethune

She spoke to the president and his wife
Like they were somebody grow'd up on her street
They liked what they heard,
made her a counselor
she ran it down to them
elevated their discourses
like a bird on a long glide upward.

The Time Began

The incandescent sky remained above where it dropped petals of life
Like one wombing mother-flower, peopling the ancient *Geb* below.
I am the bloom ritualized in the nobility of a mother's giving
Yet I am here neither by flying nor long-distance swimming.
I am here by ships laden with precious brains, senses, and talents;
I am writing the narratives of petals fallen on oppression's time.
I am confronting aliens who cared only for our shiny ebony bodies,
Though we, flexible and resilient, passed four hundred years here.

Older than the most ancient tree found in the oldest forest
Stretching back into time longer than the age of the oldest house,
We moved and moved and moved till we filled the earth with soul
And discovered pristine valleys and galloping streams,
Bubbling mountains sprayed with rays of water and sun
Trained our eyes toward the ancestral beginnings of cool.
We emerged durable, *homo sapiens*, mothers and fathers
Whose children walked until the landing at Point Comfort.

Great are the Gods

Did the gods descend or did they rise up on earth?
I see forms of Satchel Paige, Jackie Robinson, Michael Jordan,
Willie Mays, Muhammad Ali, Joe Louis, Serena Williams,
Althea Gibson, Lebron James, Jessie Owens, Jackie Joyner-Kersee,
Wilma Rudolph, Simone Biles, Jack Johnson, and I ask again,
Did the gods descend or did they rise up on earth?

Clever

Listen here young lady,
Young boy too,
I survived to make you stronger than mahogany.
I climbed a tree
Surveyed the condition
And taught myself to read
Prepared myself to lead
On the edge of Gabriel Prosser's farm
I took charge and sounded the alarm
And in the night when all was silent
I stood on the spot where his blood was shed
Counted the tattlers, one by one,
With vows so strong and clear
I had to wrestle my fear
And yet I knew what had to be done!

Heroic Mother Escaping

Barefoot and barrel-chested, she waded the water
Avoiding water moccasins and brittle thorns
Carrying her crying and hungry child on her back
Until like a mighty leathery black feline
She emerged through the grass on the northern shore.

Scene and Not Seen

Canopying palms, lazily hang, inverted hammocks,
Hovering over the manicured lawns with decorated roses
Sitting atop tables in a Savannah charmed white mansion
Where black men dressed in black serve white women juleps.

What We Shall Do

We who are wise must choose the flower that is ours
We will charge each other
We will shout out the spirit of ancestors
Fannie Lou Hamer and Marcus Garvey will appear
We shall see the image of Harriet Tubman and Nat Turner
We shall cling to Maya Angelou and John Hope Franklin,
Teaching them the love of Black Studies.
We shall sing the songs of the old black land
Calling and responding for more centuries to come
We shall praise Carter G. Woodson for correcting the script
And Alice Dunbar for writing it in the boldness of time
With formations of power, hidden weapons, and rhyme.

The People are Gods

Mainly because of masks
We talk to ancestor gods
Who can turn people into Falcons,
Chiwaras, rivers, and mountains
And can cause dancers to sing
And singers to dance
Straight up into a people's heaven.

Asphalt kings
Stretching their skinny black hands
Across the bosom of mother Africa
Reign through rain forests
Survive the Harmattan
In rainless Sahels
To break open canisters of memory.

We are the people god people
Peopling the universe
With palm-wine songs, yams, fufu,
Mango juice, peanuts, collards
Because we juju, we voodoo,
We hoodoo, and will do you, too,
Mainly because we are the people god people.

Veil

I have seen Oyo reborn
As you leave the USA
And enter Africa
At Oyo Tunji.
Deep in the South Carolina forest.

Courage Talk

Watch out brother, sister!
Racists got no humor.
History is rainy seasons
Millions of African bodies.
A phalanx, like us,
United to in mental oppression,
Stalls only to explode in sanity,

Martin Luther King

Did the king die
To up ignorance off of us?

Did the king die
To save the Sahelian masses?

Did the king die
So that black kids could live free?

Did the king die
To end police brutality?

Did the king die?

If I speak

If I speak with sad gloom
It is the mental misery
Of a prophetic doom
Which stands on our periphery.

If I speak with gloom
Memories are planted deep
In remembrance's tomb,
So, when I think, I weep.

If I speak with gloom
I am not heated with flame
Nor does my anger loom
longer than another's fame

If I speak with gloom
What I have seen and heard
Came not by a preacher's broom
Nor the sign of a Baga *Nimba* bird.

I speak with the royal diadem
Sitting high on my worried head
Like a crown, a memory gem
Bouncing on my brain's bed.

Meeting My Lover across the Ohio River

Bursting forth, exploding emotions,
Like one single blazing jacaranda,
Filled with black joy,
Unique and colorful,
I am nothing more than a flower
Singing joy, an ebony boy.

Male and female, staff and loop
Mood lingering as fog on a mountain
Producing the purest indigo,
Music from the Alake's house
Accompanied me to Freedom's side.

Can You See?

Hessians were mercs
Butchers slept in the Congo
And left their blood on the jungle leaves.
Cubans in Angola, Russians in Afghanistan,
French in the African Savannah,
Americans everywhere blazing fire.
I know that African kings are born in pomp
And queens are willing to die
Under the right circumstance.
Yet in a world of lost Benin bronzes
Ivory men heads and Dogon *nommos*,
Who can see through the painted dust
And discern the king's coming?

Black jazzers can see.
Ebony women with feet of gold can see.
Can see notes in the dusty brains that
Their mothers made,
Can see rhythms metronoming at Kwanzaa
With African queens and kings in 4-4 time.
Rockefeller and Guggenheim
Barnes and Metropolitan
Have replicas depraved and stolen
Fellini is a fake,
Sembene is for real.
So is Charles White, Aaron Douglas, Edmonia Lewis;
So is Jacob Lawrence, John Biggers, Betye Saar;
So is Ruth Waddy, Elizabeth Catlett, and Richard Wyatt.
Listen, I can hear the notes the jazzers play

Who reveal themselves when we need them,
In Berlin, Port Elizabeth, Ferguson, Watts, Paris,
London, Rio de Janeiro, and Los Angeles, too.

Child Labor

When I was eleven, picking cotton,
Character was a tall pine tree,
a mile downhill at the end of the row.
At sixteen I encountered colloques
Of character as beach palm branches
Waving a caution to me about my ways.
And when I became a restless adult
I climbed on Character's back
Like I used to scurry up Spanish mossed oaks
On the edge of the dusty cottonfield,
Riding the virtue straight into forever-ness.

Of People and Animals

We could hear the do-doop-de-doop of the horses huffs
We three, father, mother, and son,
lay in the cut with curved cutlasses in hand
fighting for posterity if we needed to
and soon the do-doop-de-doop passed
We stirred cautiously from the wet place
Moist from the morning dew
Making our way North toward the river.

Beauty as Beauty Does

Her eyes seemed translucent, almost glass-like,
Mirrors blurred by pain made it through to me
I was sick to think that she so ethereal
Had done what was necessary to free her mind
And disappear into the long narratives of self.

Keeping me from Knowledge?

I was drugged by ignorance
Kept long distances from books
Made a lonesome hermit
Frightened by my own shadow
I could neither count nor read
Yet threatened by a thousand deaths
I vowed survival like a cat cornered
Clawing, living, and reaching truth
Pouring forth from wisdom women
Matching words and cloths with nature
Everything black, red, and green
And I am forever wise and strengthened.

I Don't Feel Weary

I can take the punishment like a crocodile
My skin is soft like that of the mushrooms
That grow in nature's golden meadows,
My brain is strong, stronger than hell

My plan, a simple map, is clear
Liberation, liberation and now liberation,

I don't feel anyways weary in the run

Depression Years

Let me not gloss over my poverty,
Crumbs of bread and shavings of meat
Falling from the plates of diners
In the white-filled S and K café
I collect,
Like little dices of gold
To be shared with the depressed
Out of luck and woefully out in the cold.

On Reading

I had known symbols but could not read
I sensed squares and circles by nature
I longed to decipher words on paper
Or strange signs on cotton leaves
Like Nat Turner, who read mysteries
That woke me to the utter truth,
That white people can also die.

My Running

My feet split opened by an aged rock
Spilt traces of my blood into the sand
Where it coagulated with the tears
Of Muskogee, Cherokee, and Shawnee.

Only fifteen I had escaped
The hiding promised by the man
Who waved the dreaded cat-o-nine
 Menacingly because of my quip.

Fearful of being captured I ran toward daylight
Just long enough to outlast the hounds
And slept on the ledge near the lake
Where I was found by my mother.

She embraced me tightly and said,
"I love you for telling the truth
dat ole man ain't got no mercy,
best we keep runnin' to freedom."

And run we did!

Brutishness

Riveting sanctions against my father
Landed him without a career
Low down in a Georgia field
And we, an erstwhile family
Resurrected his dignity
Like rogue ants building an anthill.

Pivoting in the Fields of a Thousand Obstacles

Now that we are here in the gloom of this foreign land
We who have experience must throw the arrows of wisdom
Toward the young who come and keep coming along our path
Not to destroy them but to teach them how to make daggers
That will stab insanity's irrationality and pierce maggots' flesh

We who are wise must take our ancestors' flowers
Plant their seeds in the brains of our children
So that their memories re steeled with the fragrance of history
So that they see Harriet, Fannie Lou, Bethune, and Ida B. Wells

Let us not cry on the walls of distorted pivots
Turning us from heroes to sobbing weaklings who beg
Our enemies for peace and denounce Sojourner's truth.

I shall read our ancestors like fanatics read the Koran and the Bible
I shall not repudiate my history nor take away the ritual power
That gave birth to me in the time of the monstrous trouble
   we survived
I grow strong like the cotton silk tree, determined against all vile
   winds.

To what degree have they taken away the gods of Africa to destroy
   our humanity?

We who must now bind hope and despair, light and dark, sky
   and earth

Didn't Ella Baker say to us, "save the movement"
And didn't we move?
When Malcolm said fight, "didn't we take up our arms"?

When Marcus came as a spirit in the light of morning, didn't we swim like Shine from the *Titanic*?

Seedlings on infertile land looking for a new place
Where humans are not dead and their spirits flourish like the bounty of Africa,
Where humans made everything worthy of making and innovation was no hostage.
Let us look for a new place near the celestial arc
Where we can run the orbit of the sun and shout at the moon
Thinking Akhenaten's Aten must share with Atum and Ptah
And our hearts bound by the forest move to Ra's rhythms.

Entry

Ancestors laid an endless path,
muddy in the rainy season
With quicksand glue, hanging to goathide shoe.
In the dry season not hard enough
To stop the beige colored ghosts
Who stomped on the earth like horses,
Wild with lust for our blood and flesh,
Picking us off
One by one, until sixty caught
Shackled in chains.

Naked flesh cottonsilk smooth
Stirred emotions rawer than meat
Stronger than sex,
minds fogged by violent whiteness
Carrying sticks of fire
That cut the skin like knives
And drew blood like our spears.

Yet we are together here on this old path
Vowing, that while going, we will come
Again to this coastal village by the sea.

Captured and Held

The names are nothing to us
It is what happened
That strangles the imagination
And causes the brain to squeeze its hands
And the mind to swear the Great Oath.
Bimbia, Elmina, Ouidah, Goree,
All ill-tuned melodies of indignity
Poisoning us with wayward genes
Crushing us with the weight of the Bible
Pushing us down into the rat holes of hell
We remember Pointe Noire, Cape Verde,
Zanzibar and the Koran, and promise African gods
That in 400 years we will drown out all danger.

Dungeons Memory

The nasty years of human stench
Announce themselves in telling whiffs
And odor swirls intoxicate the senses.
Yet one asks curiously,
How many of these lingering spirits
hung on American oaks?
Whose eyes will never see Siala trees?
What curtain closed on Africans
Crowded like shrubbery in these hothouses of death?
What salty bodies drenched the others?
Here we pour libations for the kings and queens
Who never had a chance to wear their crowns!

Ship

What harm they meant
Standing upright on the ship, we
Lying down, looking with pity
On craven white souls without ancestors
Our floor vision undermining evil intent
Or else we threw ourselves overboard
To rid ourselves of the smell of death
In the living carcasses of a lonely race.
No pillows for our heads
No comfort of rattan and cotton for our backs
But we are strong and the strong will come again
Like the bending palms in the hurricane
We bow and bend and sprang again to life.

Boots crowd our ship's floor
With harsh crassy and uncivilized sounds
We are astounded by guttural tones
Unfamiliar to our long vowels
With lithe sweetness of sing-song.

Crossing

Sleep child of the night
Rocking on the waves
Flying toward nowhere
In the fearsome storms
That blanket our awesomeness
concealing blinking lights you see.
We count the stars, remember the galaxies, and
Know that the moon and sun
Will one day show us the way
Straight Back to Africa.

Strength

A warp of time wasted
In threats sustains the flesh with possibilities.
We are not alone as Shango, Oshun, Obatala and Ogun
Ride with us on the waves that write our names
As children of Odudua.
Olododo always wins and we become
impervious to death.

A Moment

In a faint moment almost unnoticed and unnoticeable,
A whiff, an ephemeral instance,
cloud here and gone,
I am gliding through the palmettos
Far away from here
Voices of Abeokuta in the markets
The long nights vanish into memory and
My lineage is longer than time.

Landed

No festivals here
Only old white men,
Bended and loud
Curious to death
Till money buys me—
Then.

Thinking

I am not alone
Neither is my brother
From another mother
Nor my sister from some other village
We keep our silence locked inside anguish,
More powerful than the agony of a wild ocean.

Beginning

Standing pain was never taught at the firesides
No *djelis* recounted those stories
And no *babalawos* ever spoke that sacrifice
So far removed from *Ifa*.

Yet I climb the tree of anger and hold back
My breath and voice till the whip ran its course
And the whipper died mysteriously in the woods.

Walking in Shackles

The delicate carbon colored heels of the woman
Ahead of me reminded me of the purple onions
I picked.

No, I am not amused by her gait but
I revel in the beauty of her feet
colored so dusky like mine.

On the Auction Block

She cries, her body exposed, to hounds
Who hunt her with their bloody eyes,
And who stare into her soul
Unheralded but steady like torches.

Who is to save the child girl
On the neighboring auction block?
Who does not understand what
She knows? Eyes will not crush her.
She wills herself into invisibility
Taking the pain only to fuel resolve
Until the time for avenging the ancestors!

And Now We Must Go On

She had a white dress on
Walking the sidewalkless
muddy roads of Birmingham
In the district forced on us
Monsoons came and she skiddled past mud pools
Proud, brave as the Bombingham girls
Until a pale driver drove right'
Through the biggest pool of muddy water
And dashed her dress with chocolate mud.

The Brave Never Left Us

No bravery came ever so charmingly clean
As that of the fearless black soldiers
Strapped with a thousand centuries of intelligence
And the memories of generations of skill
And the curdling courage of men battling for honor
Who could not and would not be turned around!

Under their helmets and into their uniforms
Went Thutmoses III, the greatest of all generals,
Ramses the II, User Maat Ra, Setepenra,
Toussaint L'Ouverture and Dessalines..
Menelik II, who stood up and shot down Italians
At the battle of Adwa,
Amanishakete, queen of Nubia who stopped Augustus' army,
Nzingha, mighty general of the First Chimurenga,
Boukman, the priest of power,
Shaka, the great spear of a new nation,
Nat Turner and Harriet Tubman who knew no risks too great
   to accept
In the defense of freedom,
Samory Ture, who ruled in Kankan and Futa Jallon,
Nanny of Jamaica, Zumbi of Brazil, and the bravery of Yanga
   of Mexico
Who built a fortified state of martial artists.

Let no lies be told and no myths created out of thin air
That would harass the truth of the brave soldiers
Who ate stars and moons and suns as was becoming of firm stardust.

Egun Memories

I went down to the old ancient well
Far beyond the rusty iron fence
That carved off our plot of land
From that of our closest neighbors.

A bird, bright with feathers of fluff,
Danced on a a ruddy limb of tree
Laughing, I thought, of me walking
With a bucket full of promised relief

But what the bird could not see
From on high with its beak in the air
Was that I was carrying, not water
But a pail full of ancestral memories.

Night Escape

Night moves in like a long-lost friend
Coming to claim a seat at the table
Of our misery--
Blues bought and brought
By early dusk turns black
With sadness at midnight

And resilience excelled
Only by raw courage
Carry on helping others
Struggling to move without light
Until the eternal sun rises
And we greet brightness
Moving faster now in the day.

Elevation

Years stack on top of years
Like banana leaves
Dark and tight
Without the evidence of tears

Something mighty tugs at the cables
Connecting us
I felt it first at the Oshun River
And found it again at the Schuylkill
As we threw our flowers in sacrifice,
Thousands moving in rhythms
To the upward pull of ancestors.

Sold Down the River

The drums dance in the wind
At the very thought of you
And I am trapped by the scent
Of bougainvillea along the road
Struggling to smell
The memory of your flesh,
Catching the aroma between strides,
As I walk, shackled, toward the boat.

Forty Acres and aMule

Foreign thieves stole all the land
And we cleared it for farming.
Thieves explored the Indian lands
And forced them to reservations.
Thieves kidnapped us from Africa,
And all the time our numbers grew
And we became the children of time,
Who waited for the indomitable ones,
Who only demanded then and now,
Just Forty Acres and a Mule!

Initiated in the Sea

On the mountains
In the rivers
In the forests
And on the pavements of the urban streets
I am soul deep in soul,
Living with Yemanja and Oshun
Swaying to the cool rhythms of water.

The ancestors bless our actions and relations
Start with honor and appreciation.
I am Bamileke
I am Hausa
I am a Yoruba
I am an Ewe
I am a Wolof
I am Serere
I am Igbo
I am Congo
I am Asante
I am Baule
I am Xhosa
I am Zulu
I am Peul
I am Luba
I am Kuba
I am Nuba!
I am the Escapee

He who ruins another will ruin himself

This mystery is like the dark clouds of winter
Unheated by the warmth of African summers
Going their way toward destruction.

I speak because of the force of African languages,
Like birds whispering in metaphors and tropes,
I walk the road of Robeson and Robesons before him
And enter the woods of Fannie Lou Hamer
Where the synecdoche connects to my courage
I become he who runs to escape the ruin.

Should I forget?

Should I forget
The night the white raiders burnt down my ancestral village that had existed for three hundred years?

Should I forget
The three-hundred miles march along a one-thousand-year-old trail to the sea that was soiled with black blood?

Should I forget
The cramped and suffocating holds on ships that were guaranteed to create damned claustrophobia?

If I forget I am forever cursed as an exorbitant tramp in history outfitted with ornamental shades that block out even the sun of my parents' love.

No, I shall not etch out of my mind the markings of the makings of my soul!

What Greed?

What greed must have choked humanity
Out of the bowels of monster men
Who challenged the sea,
To enslave the noble Africans
Whose coffled walk through desert,
Savanna and coastal forest,
Prepared them for four hundred years?
Like hunters finding melons on a path
We found the route to ambush greed
With the serene confidence of history
To avenge the dastardly theft of our time?

I Remember the Path

Whenever I passed along the path
My shadow followed
And my presence lingered in time
In a bleak unpainted village
On the edge of the plantation
Until I heard a muffled voice
From the hovering ancestors,
Peaceful as infinity
Beckoning me to listen.
I opened my consciousness
Remembered the tropical forest
And heard calls from myself
To liberate my people
From polluted streams of apathy

Up from the worn path
I ascended to the heights
Where courage stood overlooking
The infinite inflamed grievances
Of those in train along the path
And from the perch
I reached down the line
Rescuing my own apprehensions.
I became in time Geechee,
Angola, Igbo, Shine, John Henry,
Bluesman, Brotha, Sistah, Blood,
Skin, Black Hand Side Man,
Chief and Champ of Concrete,
Steel, and Wood, making everything.

I know my shadow lingers because
Ifa gave me my destiny before I came,
And I remember the path.

Epic Dance

I danced the Kete on the sun today
I am a moon man now on a hill
Outside a Dahomean water village

Watching history drop down
High from the memory sky
A man builds his boat
As his wife stews fish and rice
And dust bites me on cutaneous
While early moon shines bright
close to me on this young night.

Rhythms of Africa

I heard the small children singing in the school yard
They were saying
"The stream of the king's wives down from the courtyard
near the cement stoops is overflowing its banks
flooding the lost Pepsi bottles near the cigarette packets
close to the mud cakes cluttered with weeds."

I listened more closely, ear to the sky, feeling Louis Armstrong,
And heard the music of Tolson, Brooks, and Randall
Just like I had heard Bitek, Soyinka, Ndu, Ngugi, and Okai.

The rhythms were complex, but now I hear on many levels.
I am N'Orleans, Lagos, Freetown, Kinshasa, Accra, and Abidjan.

Detached

I am so sad that you are detached
From reality etched in our native pome
Like a lost cat on the runway to hell
You clamor alone, eyes searching
To belong, a long way from home.

Knowing Reincarnation

They tell me you were born
Where the rains come with music
Although your link
Is where the dazzling sun
Spawns spirits in the thickets.

You are a child of Karukera
No more beautiful waters
Flow from the source
Than the silvery curtains
Falling in Parc Aquacole.

Under the grand palm trees
Lingering over the place of youth
Like a Mother Didi
Near the granular sandy beaches
You heard the voice of the sea.

It beckoned you to come, to witness,
And you came, eyes wide open,
With ancestral blessings
Like the coming of peace,
in the mornings, near the sea.

Who is to say what spirits
mount you in the night?
Who can claim to know,
How long your soul sways
To the rhythms of Saut D'eau?

Yet captured by Ogun
You have wrestled demons
Silenced the shouters
And loudly proclaimed
"I salute! I salute!
All the loas on this day!

I Call for Oduduwa in the Belly of Odin

Oduduwa! Oduduwa! Oduduwa!
Past Odin's two ravens sent from the watchtower
We advance in Ifa's depth and seek divination
Looking for direction like birds confused by seasons.
What time is it? What weather should we expect?
Sloshing black feet through mushy swamps
We defy the coming Ragnarok without knowing
That our shiny black bodies are antithesis to fate.

Neither the children of Odin nor Thor,
Odin's son,
Can catch our quick essence, and faster feet
in the watery trails across a hundred miles.
We stand here supremely free, heads unbowed!

We defy Freya's wrath and petulance,
finding Chi-wara's fertility in the florid mountains.

I have learned, by escaping, to trick Loki
with the faux food of narcissism left by Oshun.

No transgressions blind the keen eyes of Eshu
When I call upon the names of the ancestors
And channel the thunder in Thor
To its rightful Shango of the forest.

Oduduwa, Oduduwa, Oduduwa!

I, the child of Obatala, must ponder my fate:
To be born where Uppsala's temple serves the Norse gods
While the path of pure light, measured in centuries,
Shows my feet the cosmic trail away from fear.

And I, no one's slave, fly on to my sweet Oduduwa!

On Arrival in Pennsylvania

I saw golden beams through the maple leaves
Late in the evening as I crossed the ridge,
Standing still in the place of Tubman's dream.
True of voice If ever I would dare be
A leaf fell through the sky and blessed me.

Free at last! Free at last! Free at last!

Fannie Lou Hamer

Who could tell the story better than she?
Whose pain pictured in grimaces came near hers?
What bards sat around her fire and told her things
Far in the night work before the dawn's duty?

Day dress like a sacred talisman covered her body
Nothing covered the nakedness of her courageous mind
When she shattered the myths, Americans live by
And told the plantation leaders to "Go to Hell!"

Poets

I pride myself on a gleaming history
of solaric poets and musicians.
I dance their names like Paul Laurence Dunbar,
Kgotsitsile, Tolson, Toomer, Baraka, McKay,
Like Phillis Wheatley, Gwendolyn Brooks,
Haki Madhubuti, Cullen and Mari Evans,
I soar with them in the endless curses of racism.
I dance to the funkiest music ever heard
And wrap my heart around telling verses,
Hugging Nina Simone, Billie Holiday, and Etta James
Long after the din is done and the lights are out.

Resistance and Resilience

Yesterday
I ran
I escaped
I was caught
Whipped down till the earth teared for me.

Today
I set fire to the cotton fields
I broke the cotton gin
I glued shut the shithouse
Took my woman and flew to heaven.

In the Cities after Freedom Come

We never tried to tame the cities teeming with people,
We did not seek to control the nature that raised us,
We simply strolled down the *ramblas* of towns
Floating like sensuous moving waves of human flesh
Becoming one with the mortal rhythms of our people.

Victory over Insanity

The devil gave us brain lesions for lessons
We turned them into standard behaviors
Cursed the damned demons with barbed words
And created verbal weapons of war so potent
Even after 400 years there are no decipherers.

I ain't growed up knowing nothin' bout dis
How sky stun man stuff, when the blood clouds come
Wearin' dem croaker sack breeches
That somebody picked up then throwed down
Tellin' ignant tales about yellow biddies roosting.

I see way yonder on the pregnant horizon
Yangas, houngans, *babalawos*, and *nyangas*
Shaking *ileles* rattling scrambled minds
Disassembling and reassembling *legos* on a board
To bring clarity to a puzzling syllabus of hate.

Strangers Still

I ask even now after four hundred years
What is your name?
No one ever introduced me to you or you to me.
Your infinite sounds
Create confusion in all the worlds I know
What language do you hear?
Without the drums beating out your rhythms
I am lost, at odds
With everything that my ancestors taught.

Homage to Musical Genius

Near where the old man sat with his laced shirt and torn denim pants,
A boy, not more than seven, raspberry black, with a hint of pink
Stood at first sight looking out at the ocean across from the
　fishing wharf,
Then playing mojo on a banjo with both hands like it was
　leopard skin,
Ready to escape its chained existence in the grip of a capturer.
Evening came and went like a cat into the darkness of night.
The old man was long gone to his home near the pine forest,
But the boy, blind of sight, played on hearing Africa's rhythms
Beating in the ebony crevices of his dark gray cerebrum.

The Church of St. John the Coltrane

I eased into my place on the long oak pew in the back of
  the sanctuary,
Placed my feet on the foot rest and waited for the sounds to
  burst through.

One long plaintive soloist started the sermon with *A Love Supreme*,
I repented of all my sins and confessed to myself that I had forgotten
How to take *Giant Steps* into the *Blue Train*.
I, too, learned the momentous lessons of mothers who had lost children to bondage,
Women, brave and courageous, who had slept too long without
  their men;
Men who had cried out of their heads because they could not feed
  their children.
Overwhelmed, I left the sanctuary, stood outside in San Francisco's winter,
Cattin' with Trane,
And vowed to praise the jazzmen and jazzwomen who recorded our
  victories.
Here at the sacred of sacred places bent in adherence once in a while, I
  found *Ascension*.

Rosewood

They came as they had come for three hundred years
In the dead of night,
With torchlight of the crystal North,
Remembrance of bonfire and chandeliers of death.
They came as they had always come
Fearful and scared,
That we, the set upon, would retaliate with ire.
They came to Rosewood as they had come
To Beaumont and Detroit, in groups, in rude disguises,
Disfigured like Vikings and Vandals on the hunt.
Our children, eyes wide with wonder, stood aghast
At the festival of rioters straining to be relevant;
As we, the adults, watched the flame-throwers
And protected the chaliced youthful innocence,
Ticking one more check on the damn racist board.

When Freedom Came

There was a thunderous underground
Crowded with scabrous treadmills
Waiting for the wayward runner
Who would curse eternity,
And shout death to infinity
And praise only the contemporary.

This foolishness, like a dog's tail,
Wags without wisdom's wind,
Creating a faint-hearted candidate
With a soul trapped in anonymity.

Malcolm X

Nothing passes your mortal brain
That cannot be put in verse
You urge me to maintain
Even when with weakness, I sing
Your terse, staccato melody
So deep that I strain
To understand whiteness, a curse.
Is it not so that hate
Cannot reside in love's bosom
Without generating the hemlock state
Where Sally Hemings felt racism's stain?

Young Bucks' Mysteries

In the slow, take it as you go,
lonesome walk to resilience
I say,
Cool Daddy O.
I plait the South with gritty soul
Paint the country villages black,
I tell stories late into the night
Of basalt and asphalt,
In the names of Otis Redding,
Aretha Franklin, James Brown,
Prince and Nina Simone,
I am extrusive igneous stone
Ready to make a difference
Strong as the blackest night.

Frederick Douglass

Now that years have passed, and we have found ourselves on this side of Freedom,
We have not found ourselves here by tokens of indecency stolen from this
History;
Our adornment of the turbulent adventure that puts us on the moral high Ground
Was only answered by the firmness of Douglass whose clairvoyance saw Victory
Ruffled and discovered like a special golden leaf from an unshackled Contradictory.

Mother of the Universe

Receive me, mother of the universe
I am nothing but stardust,
In your presence, and in yours only,
I bow.
Standing near a dusky palm tree
In the dark of midnight
I watch the brightest star run.
I watch it to see how it run
I wonder is that you?
Out of the well of my soul
I watched and watched
to see if it run to the Western Sky;
To my surprise
It run down to the Eastern Sky
And I knew
That I was a child of the universe
Blacker than the night
And faster than any enemy of truth!

Liberty and Freedom

I wish I had a voice like Ira Aldridge
I could sing of Peter Salem and Salem Poor
Praise Henri Christophe, James Forten
And the beautiful Elizabeth Freeman,
Whose deeds laid the chloroform floor
Upon which the Revolutionists slept
And woke to forget the chivalrous bridge
We stretched out in our quest for respect.

54th Massachusetts Glorified

They knew when they sent us to the front
That we would not return to say what was done
Our bravery they retold for generations
Though our brave hearts as tough as steel,
Still felt the weight of the bullets shot with hate
And we, standing tall like an ebony tree, fell.

Martin Delany

Who would revile,
He of the long-drum
Whose cries of alarm
Set in motion
The gnashing of teeth
In heady Pittsburgh?

They who dislike
Strength coming from
An African man
Who challenges evil,
And calls out
The death wickedness
That would steal
Children and wives
From one's own castle.

Frame of Reference

Jessie Fauset, Nella Larsen, and Zora Neale Hurston
Rose like a tsunami from the middle of the ocean
washing the lie told that black women could not write
Laying seeds for Alice Walker, Toni Cade Bambara,
Audre Lorde, Ntozake Shange, Octavia Butler
And women whose names are hidden under beds.
These daughters of the *bamboula* danced the music
Of song and myth in the Place Congo, with the Fisk Jubilee
Singers, Alvin Ailey's Company, the Hampton Choir,
and the Mighty FAMU one hundred.
They wrote their literary drumline, beating the rhythms of time
In honor of the saints who go marching on to victory!

A Thousand Miles with Chains

I walk the coffle line
Every orifice secreting blood
Or sweat.
I throw my chains
Like my uncle threw his spear
Intentionally.
I plan and I plot
Step-by-step
To avenge the ancestors
Even if it takes
A thousand years!

Abandoned?

I vow that I shall not leave my ancestors unsung;
They of the unheralded class
Shall find their names on the shrine tables.
The spent moon shall return again to them
In reds, blacks, and greens,
Ritualizing them with intense incense.
I, their son, sing their song
To the tunes of the lashing waves
Held in harmony by our spirit cables
Stretching across all seas
Connecting us to our African essence.

Home Always on My Mind

I ain't been home in mighty a while
But it is not because I've lost a mile
I have more than empty time to spare
Rustling through memories for repair.

The other day I found a torn star
In the oral traditions of my ancestor
With a note in the margins sent to me
Asking me, did I need the memory key?

Strong as the black bull of Aswan
With my mother's determination
A face relentless toward the rising sun
I needed nothing to fly home again.

Prediction

To say sorry for resistance?
No this can never be
Since I cut down a thorn tree
Infesting the gardens of our lives
I can only insinuate, not regret.

Who is to say what would have happened,
Had I not had the damned steel saw
To spill the bark and splatter the wood
Rather than listen to the growing calls for war?

But one thing I know for sure
We have not furloughed our sense of loss
We have not missed our path to victory
And we will not ever say we are sorry.

www.ingramcontent.com/pod-product-compliance
Lightning Source LLC
Chambersburg PA
CBHW070059020526
44112CB00034B/1869